THE BOOKER PRIZE HAS FINALLY REGAINED ITS CREDIBILITY?

Overview, History, Winners, And 2022 Longlist Released?

Gina Jacobs

INTRODUCTION

The associated award is presented to a writer of any country for an English-language book that was released in the United Kingdom or Ireland. The genre-spanning longlist for this year (2022) is brave and the finest conceivable reaction to the recent wave of prize closures. The Booker Prize, which was first offered to authors from the British, Irish, and Commonwealth countries in 1969, has a reputation for launching writers' careers. 2014 saw the inclusion of all English-language books published in the UK. Damon Galgut of South Africa's "The Promise" was the winner the previous year. The winner will be announced on Oct. 17 at a ceremony in London after a six-book shortlist is revealed on Sept. 6.

The Booker Prize

•   *Awarded for* - Best novel of the year written in English

•   *Presented by* - Booker, McConnell Ltd (1969–2001, Man Group (2002–2019), Crankstart (2019 onwards)

•   *Location* - Guildhall, London, England

•   **First awarded** - 1969; 53 years ago

- **Reward(s)** - £50,000

- **Website** - www.thebookerprizes.com

CHAPTER ONE
OVERVIEW OF THE BOOKER PRIZE

What Is The Booker Prize?

The Booker Prize, formerly known as the Man Booker Prize (2002–2019) and the Booker Prize for Fiction (1969–2001), is an annual literary award given to the best English-language novel that is released in the United Kingdom or Ireland. The Booker Prize winner receives widespread media attention, which typically increases sales. Only books published by Commonwealth, Irish, South African, and later Zimbabwean nationals were eligible for the prize; in 2014, the criteria were expanded to include any English-language book, a move that sparked debate. The Booker Prize Foundation appoints a seven-person panel made up of writers, librarians, literary agents, publishers, and booksellers.

The Booker Prize is a well-known literary prize in British culture, and it is celebrated with excitement. Literary critics have observed that being chosen for inclusion in the shortlist or being nominated for the "longlist" is a mark of distinction for authors. For a book that has been published in the United Kingdom or Ireland and has been translated into English, a sibling award called the International Booker Prize is given.

Administration And History

The award was originally named the Booker Prize for Fiction, but once Booker, McConnell Ltd. started sponsoring the competition in 1969, it was more often referred to as the "Booker Prize" or just the "Booker."

The financial firm Man Group took over as title sponsor after the Booker Prize Foundation took over management of the award in 2002. Man, Group decided to keep "Booker" in the award's official title. The foundation is a separate, legally recognized nonprofit organization that is supported entirely by the earnings of Booker Prize Trading Ltd, of which it is the sole stakeholder. The Booker Prize's prize money was original £21,000, but it was later increased to £50,000 in 2002 with support from the Man Group, making it one of the richest literary awards in the world.

1969–1979

Bernice Rubens won the Booker Prize for The Elected Member in 1970, making her the first woman to do so. The Booker Prize's regulations were altered in 1971; earlier, novels published before the year the prize was granted may get it retroactively. Books published in 1970 were effectively disqualified from consideration for the Booker Prize since the year of eligibility was changed in 1971 to coincide with the year of the award. The "Lost Man Booker Prize" was introduced by the Booker Prize Foundation in January 2010. The winner will be picked from a long list of 22 books that were published in 1970.

The only short story collection to be considered is Alice Munro's The Beggar Maid, which was in 1980. According to John Sutherland, who served as a judge for the 1999 award:

There is a thriving literary scene in London. Rushdie is no longer considered due to his attacks on that community. If you want to win the Booker, that is not a wise course of action. You must "be a citizen" of the US to win rewards, as Norman Mailer discovered. The fact that [Martin] Amis has never received the award is the real scandal. He has only been shortlisted once, and that was for the weakest book he has ever written, Time's Arrow. That is suspicious. With Dead Babies, he offended a lot of people, and that gets ingrained in the culture. There is also the impression that he has always had America in mind.

John Berger, the 1972 winner, and well-known Marxist expressed his disapproval of Booker McConnell during his award speech. He attributed the contemporary poverty in the Caribbean to Booker's 130 years of sugar cultivation there. Because the British Black Panther movement shared his commitment to socialism and revolution, Berger gave half of his £5,000 prize to them.

1980–1999

Earthly Powers author Anthony Burgess declined to attend the ceremony in 1980 unless he knew in advance if he had won. His novel was one of two that were predicted to win, the other being William Golding's Rites of Passage. Only 30 minutes before the presentation, the judges made their decision, awarding Golding the prize. Before the award, both books were considered favorites to win, and the dramatic "literary struggle" between two seasoned authors became front-page headlines.

John Banville, the nominee, asked for the award in a letter to The Guardian in 1981. He said he wanted to spend the money to buy all of the longlisted books in Ireland and present them to libraries, "thus ensuring that the books not only be bought but also read - a unique occurrence." Salman Rushdie's Shame and J. M. Coetzee's Life & Times of Michael K tied for first place in the 1983 prize, forcing chair of judges Fay Weldon to make a decision. Her arm was bent, and she decided on Rushdie, but as the decision was being phoned in, she changed her mind, according to Stephen Moss in The Guardian.

The English Patient by Michael Ondaatje and Sacred Hunger by Barry Unsworth were tied for first place in 1992, according to the jury. In response, the foundation established a rule requiring the jury to only bestow awards on a single author or book. When Trainspotting made the longlist in 1993, two of the judges threatened to leave, therefore Irvine Welsh's book was removed from the shortlist to appease them. Later on, the book would win praise from critics; now, it is regarded as Welsh's finest work.

How Late It Was, How Late by James Kelman was selected as the 1994 Booker Prize winner, and it turned out to be one of the most contentious decisions in the award's history. One of the judges, Rabbi Julia Neuberger, termed it "a shame" and left the ceremony, later calling the book "trash." WHSmith's marketing manager called the prize "an embarrassment to the entire book trade." The following week, Waterstones in Glasgow only sold 13 copies of Kelman's book.

Richard Gott, the literary editor of The Guardian, referred to the award as "a significant and dangerous iceberg in the sea of British culture that serves as a symbol of its current malaise" in 1994, citing the absence of objective criteria and the exclusion of American authors. The awarding of The God of Small Things by Arundhati Roy in 1997 caused some controversy.

The previous year's Booker judge's chair, Carmen Callil, referred to it as an "execrable" novel and declared on television that it shouldn't even have made the shortlist. Following the judges' rejection of Bernard MacLaverty's shortlisted book because they claimed he was "a superb short-story writer and that Grace Notes was three short tales linked together," Booker Prize chairman Martyn Goff claimed Roy won because nobody complained.

2000–Present

Before 2001, the long list of nominees for each year was kept a secret. The reward was selected by "who knows who, who's sleeping with who, who's supplying drugs to who, who's married to who, whose turn it is," according to A. L. Kennedy, a judge in 1996, was branded "a load of crooked rubbish" in 2001.

The Oxford Brookes University Library now serves as the permanent home for the Booker Prize records, which date from 1968 to the present. The Archive, which covers the administrative history of the Prize from 1968 to the present, gathers a variety of materials, such as correspondence, publicity materials, copies of both the Longlists and the Shortlists, meeting minutes, photographs, and materials related to the awards banquet (letters of invitation, guest lists, seating plans). Certain kinds of content are subject to ten- or twenty-year embargoes; examples include all documentation of the judging procedure and the Longlist before 2002.

Irish and Indian authors competed for the Booker Prize alternately between 2005 and 2008. This trend was started by "outsider" John Banville in 2005 when his book The Sea was unexpectedly chosen as the winner. Boyd Tonkin, the literary editor of The Independent, famously denounced the choice as "possibly the most perverse decision in the history of the award," and rival author Tibor Fischer derided Banville's victory. India's Kiran Desai won in 2006. A jury that was extremely divided over Ian McEwan's book On Chesil Beach led to Anne Enright's win in 2007. The next year, it was India's turn once more. Sebastian Barry, an Enright fellow Irishman, lost to Aravind Adiga by a razor-thin margin.

In the past, the Booker Prize recipient had to be a resident of Zimbabwe, the Republic of Ireland, or the Commonwealth of Nations. It was stated on 18 September 2013 that future Booker Prize awards would consider authors from anywhere in the world, so long as their work was in English and published in the UK. In literary circles, this modification caused some controversy. Former winners A. S. Byatt and John Mullan claimed that the prize ran the risk of losing its integrity, although former judge A. L. Kennedy supported the adjustment. After this extension, American Paul Beatty became the first winner who did not hail from the Commonwealth, Ireland, or Zimbabwe 2016. The next year, George

Saunders, another American, took first place. Publishers fought to undo the change in 2018, claiming that incorporating American authors will homogenize the field and reduce diversity and opportunity for readers worldwide, especially in America, to discover "excellent novels that haven't already been publicly celebrated."

Early in 2019, Man Group declared that the reward for this year would be the last of the eighteen they have sponsored. The award was then taken up by a new sponsor, Crankstart, a charity organization led by Sir Michael Moritz and his wife, Harriet Heyman, for five years with the possibility of extension. The Booker Prize was modified to its current name.

The foundation's jury, led by Peter Florence, split the 2019 prize and gave it to two authors in violation of a 1993 regulation, despite receiving a clear warning not to do so. Florence defended the choice by saying: "It ultimately came down to a discussion about the guidelines with the Booker Prize director. And we were told rather adamantly that the regulations forbid having more than one winner. However, because the jury was controlled entirely based on consensus, we concluded that it was our option to break the law this year and divide the reward to honor two winners." The two were Canadian author Margaret Atwood for The Testaments and British author Bernardine Evaristo for her book Girl, Woman, Other. Evaristo's victory marked the first time a black woman had won the Booker, and Atwood's victory made her the oldest winner at age 79.

Judging

An advisory group composed of a writer, two publishers, a literary agency, a bookseller, a librarian and a chairperson chosen by the Booker Prize Foundation is formed to begin the process of choosing the prize winner. The judging panel is then chosen by the advisory committee, except for a few rare cases when a judge may be chosen twice. Leading literary critics, authors, scholars, and prominent public people are chosen to serve as judges.

Many people disagree with the Booker judging procedure and the idea that a "best book" is selected by a select group of literary insiders. In response to this, The Guardian established the "Not the Booker Prize," which readers vote for. The concept that a "book of the year" can be judged annually by a group of people - judges who have to read nearly a book a day - is preposterous, as is the notion that this is any manner of recognizing a writer, according to author Amit Chaudhuri.

Early October typically sees the Guildhall in London host a formal banquet where the winner is declared. With COVID-19 pandemic restrictions in place, the winner ceremony was televised from The Roundhouse in November of 2020. This was accomplished with the BBC's assistance.

British Empire's Legacy

Luke Strongman, a scholar, observed that the 1969 Booker prize regulations, which restricted the winners to English-language novelists from Great Britain or former British Empire countries, strongly implied that the prize's goal was to strengthen ties between the countries that had all once belonged to the empire. Something to Answer For, the first book to win the Booker Prize in 1969, was about the mishaps of an Englishman in Egypt in the 1950s, while British influence in Egypt was waning. According to Strongman, many of the Booker Prize winners have indulged in imperial nostalgia, and the majority of works that have won the award have dealt in some manner with the legacy of the British Empire. However, as new identities have emerged in the former colonies of the empire and with them, "culture after the empire," many of the prize-winning books have over time reflected the altered power dynamics. Although successive British authorities' attempts to shape "the locals" into their image fell short, they nonetheless significantly and irreversibly altered the cultures of the colonized, a theme that numerous non-white Booker prize winners have explored in a variety of ways.

Winners

FORMAT: YEAR, AUTHOR,   TITLE,   GENRE(S). COUNTRY

1. 1969,   P. H. Newby,   Something to Answer For,   Novel,   United Kingdom

2. 1970,   Bernice Rubens,   The Elected Member, Novel,   United Kingdom

3. 1971,   V. S. Naipaul,   In a Free State,   Novel, United Kingdom

Trinidad and Tobago

4. 1972,   John Berger G.,   Experimental, novel, United Kingdom

5. 1973, J. G. Farrell, The Siege of Krishnapur, Novel, United Kingdom

Ireland

6. 1974, Nadine Gordimer, The Conservationist, Novel, South Africa

, Stanley Middleton, Holiday, Novel, United Kingdom

7. 1975, Ruth Prawer Jhabvala, Heat and Dust Historical, novel, United Kingdom

Germany

8. 1976, David Storey Saville, Novel, United Kingdom

9. 1977, Paul Scott, Staying On, Novel, United Kingdom9. 1978, Iris Murdoch, The Sea, the Sea, Philosophical, novel, United Kingdom, Ireland

10. 1979, Penelope Fitzgerald, Offshore, Novel, United Kingdom

11. 1980,   William Golding, Rites of Passage,   Novel, United Kingdom

12. 1981,   Salman Rushdie,   Midnight's Children, Magic realism,   United Kingdom

13. 1982,   Thomas Keneally, Schindler's Ark, Biographical, novel,   Australia

14. 1983,   J. M. Coetzee,   Life & Times of Michael K,   Novel,   South Africa

15. 1984,   Anita Brookner,   Hotel du Lac,   Novel, United Kingdom

16. 1985,   Keri Hulme, The Bone People, Mystery novel, New Zealand

17. 1986,   Kingsley Amis,   The Old Devils,   Comic novel, United Kingdom

18. 1987,   Penelope Lively,   Moon Tiger, Novel,
    United Kingdom

19. 1988,   Peter Carey, Oscar, and Lucinda,
    Historical novel,   Australia

2o. 1989,   Kazuo Ishiguro,   The Remains of the Day,
    Historical novel,   United Kingdom

21. 1990,   A. S. Byatt, Possession, Historical, novel,
United Kingdom

22. 1991,   Ben Okri,   The Famished Road,   Magic
realism,   Nigeria

23. 1992,   Michael Ondaatje, The English Patient,
    Historiographic metafiction,   Canada

    Barry Unsworth,   Sacred Hunger,   Historical
novel,   United Kingdom

24. 1993,   Roddy Doyle,   Paddy Clarke Ha Ha Ha,
    Novel,   Ireland

25. 1994,   James Kelman,   How Late It Was, How Late, Stream of consciousness, United Kingdom

26. 1995,   Pat Barker, The Ghost Road   War, novel, United Kingdom

27. 1996,   Graham Swift,   Last Orders, Novel, United Kingdom

28. 1997,   Arundhati Roy,   The God of Small Things, Novel,   India

29. 1998,   Ian McEwan,   Amsterdam, Novel, United Kingdom

30. 1999,   J. M. Coetzee,   Disgrace,   Novel, South Africa

31. 2000,   Margaret Atwood, The Blind Assassin, Historical novel,   Canada

32. 2001,   Peter Carey, True History of the Kelly Gang, Historical novel,   Australia

33. 2002,   Yann Martel,   Life of Pi,   Fantasy and adventure novel,   Canada

34. 2003,   DBC Pierre, Vernon God Little, Black comedy,   Australia

35. 2004,   Alan Hollinghurst, The Line of Beauty, Historical novel,   United Kingdom

36. 2005,   John Banville,   The Sea,   Novel, Ireland

37. 2006,   Kiran Desai, The Inheritance of Loss, Novel, India

38. 2007,   Anne Enright,   The Gathering,   Novel, Ireland

39. 2008,   Aravind Adiga,   The White Tiger,   Novel,
     India

40. 2009,   Hilary Mantel,   Wolf Hall,   Historical
novel,   United Kingdom

41. 2010,   Howard Jacobson, The Finkler Question,
     Comic novel,   United Kingdom

42. 2011,   Julian Barnes,   The Sense of an Ending,
     Novel,   United Kingdom

43. 2012,   Hilary Mantel,   Bring Up the Bodies,
     Historical novel,   United Kingdom

44. 2013,   Eleanor Catton,   The Luminaries,
     Historical novel,   New Zealand

45. 2014,   Richard Flanagan, The Narrow Road to the
Deep North, Historical novel,   Australia

46. 2015,   Marlon James,   A Brief History of Seven Killings,   Historical/experimental novel,   Jamaica

47. 2016,   Paul Beatty, The Sellout, Satirical novel,   United States

48. 2017,   George Saunders,   Lincoln in the Bardo,   Historical/experimental novel,   United States

49. 2018,   Anna Burns, Milkman,   Novel,   United Kingdom

50. 2019,   Margaret Atwood, The Testaments   Novel,   Canada

Bernardine Evaristo,   Girl, Woman, Other,   Experimental novel,   United Kingdom

51. 2020,   Douglas Stuart,   Shuggie Bain,   Novel,   United Kingdom,

United States

52. 2021,   Damon Galgut,   The Promise,   Novel,
South Africa

53. 2022, SEE NOMINEES BELOW

Unique Awards

A "Booker of Bookers" Prize was presented in 1993 to commemorate the award's 25th birthday. Midnight's Children by Salman Rushdie, the 1981 winner, was selected by three former prize judges, Malcolm Bradbury, David Holloway, and W. L. Webb, as "the best novel out of all the winners."

The Man Booker Prize established the "Best of Beryl" award in 2006 in honor of author Beryl Bainbridge, who had had five nominations but just one victory. The award reportedly counts toward the Booker Prize. A Big Adventure, Every Man for Himself, The Bottle Factory Outing, The Dressmaker, and Master Georgie were the films nominated; Master Georgie took home the prize. In a similar vein, The Best of the Booker was given out in 2008 to commemorate the award's 40th birthday. Midnight's Children once again took first place after the public voted on a shortlist of six finalists.

No novel published in 1970 could receive the Booker Prize since the nature of the Prize was changed in 1971 to give it to novels published in that year rather than the year before. This was fixed in 2010 when J. G. Farrell's Troubles received the "Lost Man Booker Prize." The Golden Man Booker Prize was given out in 2018 to commemorate the publication's 50th year. A group of judges chose one book from each era: Mantel's Wolf Hall, Saunders' Lincoln in the Bardo, Moon Tiger by Lively in 1987, The English Patient by Ondaatje in 1992, and In a Free State by Naipaul in 1971. The English Patient was voted the winner by the general public.

Nomination

Since 2014, based on their longlisting history, each publisher's label is permitted to submit a certain number of titles (previously they could submit two). Publishers who have not been longlisted may submit one title; publishers who have been longlisted once or twice in the previous five years may submit two; publishers who have been longlisted three times or more may submit three, and publishers who have been longlisted five times or more may submit four.

Additionally, if entrants submit new titles, prior prize winners are automatically taken into account. Books may also be called in; publishers may ask judges to consider additional titles in addition to those previously submitted in writing. The judges have typically considered about 130 works per year since the year 2000.

Awards Connected To Translated Works

The Man Booker International Prize was established in 2005 and is a unique award for which any writer who is still alive around the globe is eligible. It used to be awarded every two years to a living author of any country for a body of work that had been published in English or was widely accessible in an English translation until 2015. The prize was drastically changed in 2016 and is now granted annually to a single book in English translation. The winner's book receives a £50,000 reward that is split equally between the author and the translator.

The Booker-Open Russia Literary Prize, commonly referred to as the Russian Booker Prize, was established in 1992 as a Russian equivalent of the Booker Prize. The Man Asian Literary Prize is an annual literary award presented to the best novel by an Asian author, either written in English or translated into English and published in the previous calendar year. It was created in 2007 by Man Group plc.

On the final Saturday of the festival, a Booker event is held as a part of The Times' Literature Festival in

Cheltenham. A shortlist of four works from a certain year before the Booker prize's inception is discussed by four guest speakers/judges, and a winner is selected. In contrast to the real Man Booker (1969–2014), authors from beyond the Commonwealth are also taken into consideration. Cry, the Beloved Country by Alan Paton won the 2008 award for 1948, defeating The Naked and the Dead by Norman Mailer, The Heart of the Matter by Graham Greene, and The Loved One by Evelyn Waugh. The Thirty-Nine Steps by John Buchan, Of Human Bondage by W. Somerset Maugham, Psmith, Journalist by P. G. Wodehouse, and The Voyage Out were all beaten by Ford Madox Ford's The Good Soldier in 2015. (Virginia Woolf).

CHAPTER TWO

FINALLY, THE BOOKER PRIZE HAS RESTORED ITS CREDIBILITY?

With the abrupt elimination of the Blue Peter Prize and the Costa Book Awards during the past few weeks, literary awards have been falling like ninepins. Happily, the Booker Prize has provided us with its customary "Booker's Dozens" of 13 books that have been shortlisted for the award, offering the finest answer to the recent wave of prize cancellations.

But by offering us a longlist that emphasizes the unconventional, the experimental, and the underappreciated—exactly what the Booker should (but doesn't always do—they have provided a brilliant riposte to what threatens to become a lily-livered publishing atmosphere. It appears that the Booker Prize has restored its credibility following the scandal in 2019 where Margaret Atwood and Bernardine Evaristo were made to share the award.

First of all, it should be noted that the judges have mainly shunned big names, confident enough to tell readers what they believe is worth a shot rather than attempting to spark their attention by sprinkling in a few fan favorites.

There is no room for Jonathan Franzen's heavy-handed Crossroads, often considered the commander-in-chief of the American Republic of letters. Both Jennifer Egan's critically acclaimed follow-up to A Visit from the Goon Squad, The Candy House, and Ian McEwan's similarly lengthy and ambitious Lessons are missing.

CHAPTER THREE

LEILA MOTTLEY AND ELIZABETH STROUT UP FOR BOOKER FICTION PRIZE

2022 Booker Prize Longlist

Best-selling Among the 13 authors competing for the renowned Booker Prize for fiction is American novelists Leila Mottley, Elizabeth Strout, and Karen Joy Fowler. The symphony of daily lives "Oh William!" by Strout, "Booth," by Fowler, and Mottley's debut novel "Nightcrawler," which is set in Oakland, are three of the six American books on the longlist for the 50,000 pounds ($60,000) prize. Additionally, authors from Zimbabwe, Sri Lanka, Britain, and Ireland are on the list that was released on Tuesday.

Out of 169 novels that publishers submitted for consideration, five judges made their decisions. The selection, according to the committee's head, Neil MacGregor, a former director of the British Museum, "includes the story, fable and parable, fantasy, mystery, meditation, and thriller." Many of the books, according to him, wrestle with "the elusive nature of truth" and contain narratives that are motivated by "long histories of war and injustice."

1.   By Noviolet Bulawayo's, Glory

The second book by the well-known Zimbabwean author dramatizes the recent political unrest in a way akin to Animal Farm. In "the oddest book of 2022," according to the Telegraph review, Mugabe is a horse and his wife is a donkey.

2.   By Hernán Diaz, Trust

This devious hall of mirrors of a book uses a variety of literary devices, including biography, diary, and novel-within-novel, to create a beguilingly paradoxical portrayal of a shady Wall Street financier who thrives despite the Great Depression.

3.   The Trees, A Work By Percy Everett

In this comic blend of political satire, zombie horror, and whodunit, a serial murderer seeks vengeance on the families of individuals who were accountable for the actual hanging of 14-year-old Emmett Till in Mississippi in 1955.

4.   *Booth By Karen Joy Fowler*

A hilarious depiction of a real-life, rowdy American theatrical family, led by the brilliant Shakespearean actor Junius Brutus Booth, who was also a crazed bigamist, and embarrassed by his son John, who killed Abraham Lincoln.

5.   *Alan Garner's Treacle Walker*

Alan Garner, a British fantasy author nominated for "Treacle Walker," is the oldest Booker nominee ever at 87. In one of Garner's best works, a little kid is introduced to a bizarre world where the dead may speak and characters from his favorite comic books come to life through a chance encounter with a mysterious rag-and-bone guy.

6.   *Oh, William! By Elizabeth Strout*

This moving and bitingly amusing follow-up to My Name Is Lucy Barton, which was also Booker-longlisted, sends elderly Lucy on a road trip with her ex-husband to illustrate why their intense love wasn't enough to keep them together. Strout is nominated for "Oh William!" and is the most well-known author on the 13-person list.

7.   Shehan Karunatilaka's The Seven Moons Of Maali Almeida

A war photographer dies horribly and then tries to change events in Sri Lanka from the afterlife in this hilarious comedy set against the backdrop of the Sri Lankan Civil War.

8.   Claire Keegan's Small Things Like These

The smallest novel on the list is Keegan's 116-page Small Things Like These, which takes place in a small Irish town in the days leading up to Christmas 1985. By concentrating on a man who risks his affluent life to end his community's complicity in the atrocities occurring in the Irish Magdalene laundries, this short, fable-like novella finds a creative method to address the well-worn subject matter.

9.   By Graeme Macrae Burnet, Case Study

This is as bewilderingly clever and fascinating as Burnet's Booker-nominated His Bloody Project, which is framed as the history of a forgotten celebrity psychiatrist from the 1960s and includes excerpts from one of his patients' journals.

10.   Audrey Magee's *The Colony*

In a haunting novel that provides both direct and oblique commentary on The Troubles, an English painter and a French linguist settle on a small island off the coast of Ireland in 1979, not always to the residents' delight.

11.   *Maddie Mortimer's Maps Of Our Spectacular Body*

This unsettling experimental piece centers on a lady reflecting on her life while battling terminal cancer. She battles for control of her narrative against an intrusive, interfering narrator who might be a metaphor for the illness itself.

12.   *Nightcrowling By Leila Mottley*

The 20-year-old Mottley, the youngest-ever Booker longlist, takes inspiration from her harrowing tale of a sex worker who turns into a media target after being sexually abused by police from a true incident in her California hometown. "Nightcrawler," which she wrote while still a teen, has received excellent reviews and was chosen for Oprah's Book Club.

13.   *After Sappho By Selby Wynn Schwartz*

This book's introduction weaves together "speculative biographies" of several early feminists and self-described Sapphists, illuminatingly tampering with the lives of Virginia Woolf, Gertrude Stein, and others.

CHAPTER FOUR

BOOKER PRIZE NOMINEES WHO ARE MAINSTREAM AMERICAN AUTHORS

American novelists make up six of the 13 authors competing for the coveted British literary award, together with authors from Zimbabwe, Britain, and Ireland. The six American authors nominated for this year's Booker Prize were announced in a news release on Tuesday. They include Elizabeth Strout, Karen Joy Fowler, and Leila Mottley.

Leila Mottley for "Nightcrawler," a best-seller about a desperate Black teen in California who becomes involved in a sex-trafficking ring, and Karen Joy Fowler for "Booth," a fictional family picture of the clan around John Wilkes Booth, who assassinated Abraham Lincoln.

Hernan Diaz for "Trust," Selby Wynn Schwartz for "After Sappho," and Percival Everett for "The Trees" are the other Americans nominated. One of the most prominent literary prizes in the world, the Booker Prize, is granted annually to the author of an English-language book that has been released in Britain or Ireland. With recent winners including Margaret Atwood, Bernardine Evaristo, and Douglas Stuart, it is renowned for capping literary careers and launching new literary stars.

Before 2014, the prize was exclusively available to writers from Britain, Ireland, the Commonwealth, and Zimbabwe. However, ever since it was opened to writers of any nationality, the British literary establishment has frequently lamented the predominance of American writers on the Booker list. Although the nominees also include NoViolet Bulawayo from Zimbabwe and Shehan Karunatilaka from Sri Lanka, as well as three British and two Irish authors, the announcement on Tuesday, is certain to rekindle those worries.

A pioneering writer of children's fantasy novels in the 1960s and 1970s, Alan Garner, 87, is one of the British authors on the list and is credited by the Booker as being its oldest contender ever. The subject matter of the nominated books is incredibly varied. The nominations for "Glory," an animal fable that chronicles the fall of a dictatorship, come from Bulawayo; "Maps of our Spectacular Bodies," a book whose dual narrators are a dying mother and cancer that is taking her life, are from Maddie Mortimer.

In a news release announcing the nominees, Neil MacGregor, the former director of the British Museum and this year's chair of judges, underscored the variety by stating that the novels comprised "narrative, fable and parable, fantasy, meditation, and thriller." However, he claimed that two overarching themes stood out: the elusive nature of truth and how "individual lives are formed and defined by long historical processes." The real issue of many of these writings, according to MacGregor, is how much we can trust the spoken or written word.

The six-title shortlist will be revealed on September 6, after the Booker judges—who also include the critic Shahidha Bari and the author Alain Mabanckou—have reread all of the nominees. The winning novel will be revealed on October 17 at an event in London, with the author receiving a prize of 50,000 pounds, or roughly $60,000.

CONCLUSION

One can already hear a panic-induced approach of play-it-safe conservatism starting to take hold in the publishing industry as corporate sponsors appear to be growingly unhappy about paying money to be associated with books that aren't certainly going to be surefire hits. The risk is that publishers will focus on cozy, undemanding works that are carefully crafted to attract a sizable readership in the hopes of conserving the prizes we still have or balancing the losses associated with the cancellation of prizes and concomitant loss of publicity. ***DO LEAVE YOUR REVIEW AFTER READING THIS BOOK!***

Printed in Great Britain
by Amazon

35693721R00030